# BOSTON

Unforgettable Vintage Images of an All-American City

# Note from the Publisher

Royalties from the sale of this book will be paid into a fund for historic preservation to be administered by Arcadia Publishing. We envisage that proceeds from the fund will go toward supporting local history projects in the community. For further details, please contact us at Arcadia's Midwest office.

# BOSTON

Unforgettable Vintage Images of an All-American City

ARCADIA

First published 2000.

Published by:
Arcadia Publishing, Inc.
3470 N. Lincoln Ave., Suite 410
Chicago, IL 60657

Typesetting and origination by Tempus Publishing, Inc.
Printed and bound in Great Britain.

Library of Congress Number: 00-104647
ISBN 0-7385-0727-X

For all general information contact Arcadia Publishing at:
Telephone 843-853-2070
Fax 843-853-0044
E-Mail sales@arcadiapublishing.com

For customer service and orders:
Toll-Free 1-888-313-2665

Visit us on the internet at http://www.arcadiaimages.com

# CONTENTS

# ACKNOWLEDGMENTS

*Arcadia would like to thank the following individuals and groups for their contributions.*

## AUTHORS

| | |
|---|---|
| Cynthia Chalmers Bartlett | *Beacon Hill* |
| Paul Buchanan | *Milton* |
| Frank Cheney | *Boston in Motion* |
| | *Trolleys Under the Hub* |
| Norman E. Down | *Saugus* |
| Richard A. Duffy | *Arlington* |
| Laurie Evans-Daly | *Framingham* |
| Joanne S. Foley | *Lynn* |
| David C. Gordon | *Framingham* |
| John M. Grove | *Norwood* |
| Greer Hardwicke | *Brookline* |
| William P. Marchione, Ph.D | *Allston-Brighton* |
| | *The Charles: A River Transformed* |
| | *Italian Americans of Greater Boston: A Proud Tradition* |
| Christopher R. Mathias | *Nahant* |
| Roger Reed | *Brookline* |
| Stephen J. Schier | *Peabody* |
| Kenneth C. Turino | *Nahant* |
| | *Peabody* |
| Anthony Mitchell Sammarco | *Boston: A Century of Progress* |
| | *Boston in Motion* |
| | *Boston's Back Bay* |
| | *Boston's Harbor Islands* |
| | *Boston's North End* |
| | *Boston's South End* |
| | *Boston's West End* |
| | *Cambridge* |
| | *Charlestown* |
| | *Dorchester* |
| | *East Boston* |
| | *The Great Boston Fire of 1872* |
| | *Hyde Park* |
| | *Jamaica Plain* |
| | *Milton* |
| | *Roxbury* |
| | *South Boston* |
| | *Trolleys Under the Hub* |

# HISTORICAL ORGANIZATIONS

Arlington Historical Society
Atlanticare Hospital
Baker Library, Harvard University
Beacon Hill News
Boston Athenaeum
Boston College
Boston Gas Company
Boston Globe
Boston Herald
Boston Landmarks Commission
Boston Public Library
Bostonian Society
Brighton-Allston Historical Society
Brookline Preservation Commission
Brookline Public Library
Cambridge Health Alliance
Cambridge Historical Commission
Cambridge Public Library
Carney Hospital
Center for Italian Culture
Charlestown Branch, Boston Public Library
Charlestown Patriot
Classical High School
Congregation Kehillath Israel
Dante Alighieri Society
Doric Dames of the Massachusetts State House
Dudley Street Branch, Boston Public Library
East Boston Branch, Boston Public Library
East Boston Savings Bank
Faulkner Hospital
Fine Arts Department, Boston Public Library
First Parish Church, Charlestown
Forbes House Museum
Forest Hills Cemetery
Framingham Historical Society
Francis Ouimet Society
Frederick Law Olmstead Site
Friends of Mount Auburn Cemetary

# HISTORICAL ORGANIZATIONS *continued*

Gazette Publications
General Electric Company
Gettysburg National Military Park
Gibson House Museum
Grove Hall Branch, Boston Public Library
Harriet McCormack Center for the Performing Arts
Harvard University
Heritage Education
Hyde Park Branch, Boston Public Library
Hyde Park Historical Society
Immigrant City Archives of Lowell
Italian Home for Children
Jamaica Plain Branch, Boston Public Library
Jamaica Plain Historical Society
John F. Kennedy Library
John J. Burns Library
Lawton Vernwood Press
Lemuel Shattuck Hospital
Library of Congress
Longyear Museum and Society
Lynn English High School
Lynn GAR
Lynn Historical Society
Lynn Museum
Lynn Public Library
Massachusetts General Hospital
Massachusetts Historical Society
Milford, New Hampshire Historical Society
Milton Historical Society
Mt. Carmel Lodge
Museum of Afro-American History
Museum of Transportation
Nahant Historical Society
Nahant Public Library
National Park Service
New England Baptist Hospital
Newburyport Public Library
North End Branch, Boston Public Library
North Shore Jewish Historical Society
Norwood Historical Society Old South Meeting House Association

# HISTORICAL ORGANIZATIONS *continued*

Old West Church
Park School
Peabody Essex Museum Library
Peabody Historical Society
Public Facilities Department, City of Boston
Revere Historical Society
Rivers School
Robbins Library
Roslindale Historical Society
Roxbury High School
Saugus Public Library
Shepley, Bulfinch, Richardson & Abbot
Society for the Preservation of New England Antiquities
Somerville Public Library
South Boston Branch, Boston Public Library
South Boston Historical Society
South End Branch, Boston Public Library
South End Historical Society
Sports Film Lab
St. Georges Greek Orthodox Church
St. John's Prep, Danvers
St. Stephens Episcopal Church
Symmes Hospital
Urban College of Boston
Victorian Society, New England Chapter
Watertown Free Public Library
West End Branch, Boston Public Library
West End Historical Association
West Ender
West Roxbury High School
West Roxbury Historical Society
Yale University Art Gallery

# INTRODUCTION

Whether it be a chapter in an American history book, a Longfellow poem, an episode of "Cheers," or a walk along the "Freedom Trail," history texts and popular culture have already defined the images of Boston to an outsider. Here at Arcadia, our goal has been to illuminate the images of Boston that history and popular culture have ignored. It is not the stores along Washington Street that define Boston, but rather the stories buried beneath. It is not the modern buildings that house international businesses that define Boston, but rather the ashes of the Great Fire of 1872 from which these buildings were built. Boston is not so much in the faces of Paul Revere, John Adams, and Edgar Allen Poe as it is in the anonymous volunteer firefighters in 1872, the shadows of the thousands of Bostonians who gave their lives in the Revolutionary War, the War of 1812, the Civil War, the two World Wars, the Korean War, and the Vietnam War. The true images of Boston cannot be found in galleries or textbooks, but rather in faded pictures buried in cardboard boxes in the corner of the attic or buried in a dresser drawer.

The *Images of America* series began with the idea of preserving the histories of America's communities and the hope that such an idea would find a market. The publication of our 1,000th book is a statement of the extraordinary civic pride felt in Boston, in Massachusetts, and all across the United States. The authors of the 31 books from which the photographs in this *Best Images of Boston* book have been drawn are professors, archivists, historians, and friends, all from Boston. The images collected in these works are from Boston families, public libraries, universities, and neighborhood historical societies. These are the people and organizations which keep Boston's past alive and it is in their love for their city that reveals its promise for the future.

Mike Spiegel
Editor, Arcadia Publishing

*Facts about Boston*

- Since its founding in 1630, Boston has grown to about 40 times its original size.
- Boston was incorporated as a city in 1822—47 years after the start of the Revolutionary War.
- The population of Boston is approximately 574,283.
- The population of Metropolitan Boston is approximately 3,227,707.
- Alexander Graham Bell invented the telephone in Boston in 1876, four years after the Great Fire.
- Modern anesthesia, in the form of ether, was invented at Massachusetts General Hospital in 1846.
- As a city, Boston has the third largest Roman Catholic population behind Los Angeles and Chicago.

# One
# BUSINESS AND
# INDUSTRY

A group of men pose on the poop deck of the *Alma Cummings*. These remarkably well-dressed shipbuilders, complete with derbies, were part of a breed of builders that were fast disappearing by the turn of the century. (Courtesy of the BPL.)

John M. Brooks, a noted shipbuilder, shipwright, and caulker, stands in the doorway of his office at 334 Border Street. His shipyard was once a part of McKay's, where he served as a foreman. (Courtesy of the BPL.)

An interior photograph of the machine shop at the Atlantic Works shows men working on machinery that would be used on ships.

The shops and yard of the Lockwood Manufacturing Company were managed by A.H. Folger and were on the waterfront, just south of Maverick Square.

The Chelsea Bridge connected East Boston and Chelsea across the Chelsea Creek. A group of men stand on the bridge as wood risers are floated on a barge under the bridge to begin repairs in 1914. (Courtesy of SPNEA.)

Nason's Fruit and Provision Store was at the corner of Bartlett and Green Streets. Mr. Nason (on the left) and a clerk stand in front of the shop, a typical corner grocery store of the late nineteenth century. George Nason, son of the owner, and his friend Albert Briggs sit on the seat of the delivery wagon for orders that were dispatched throughout Charlestown. (Courtesy of the BPL.)

A portion of Wood Island Park was taken for the Boston Municipal Airport in 1922. After one year of construction "the airfield was a 189-acre cinder patch, with two landing strips and three hangers." A two-seater "Douglas," with a 600-horsepower Curtiss Conqueror motor, is shown here at the airport in 1932.

The *Glory of the Seas* was built in 1869 by Donald McKay, who wears a top hat as he gazes up at the ship. Built on speculation, the *Glory of the Seas* continued in service until 1923, but was unfortunately the last clipper ship built by McKay at his shipyard in East Boston. (Courtesy of the BPL.)

15

Woodbury & Company was founded in 1850 and was located at the corner of Sumner and Lewis Streets. (Courtesy of SPNEA.)

Local delivery of ice by the Jamaica Pond Ice Company was delivered to residences for use in iceboxes, which were wood chests lined with zinc that allowed food to stay fresh for a day or two. Here two delivery men using ice tongs hold blocks of ice that had been cut to the proper size for the new iceboxes. If the block proved too large, it could be reduced in size with an ice pick. (Courtesy of the BPL.)

This is another view of the popular boathouse on Flax Pond.

Men stand in the doorways to a boot and shoe shop at the corner of Lewis and North Streets in 1860. (Courtesy of the BPL.)

Weaving Axminster rugs at the Roxbury Carpet Company was serious business. An Axminster rug was a high-pile, quality carpet offered in a wide range of patterns and colors. They were popular in the first half of the twentieth century. (FHS Collections.)

The abundance of good clay along the banks of the Waters River was ideal for the manufacturing of utilitarian pottery in Peabody and Danvers. Shown in the warehouse interior are examples of various finished products.

This interior view of A.D. Mowry & Company's Pharmacy reveals a well-stocked apothecary shop that filled not just prescriptions but also had a "hot and cold" fountain for beverages on the right. Located at 329 Warren Street, Mowry's also carried confectionaries, stationery, fancy soaps, toiletries, fancy goods, and perfumes. (Courtesy of William Dillon.)

Devine's Lunch, later known as the State Luncheonette, was located near the railroad tracks and Central Street. The building is a sub shop today. (Photograph courtesy of the Down Collection.)

"The Professor" was an intimate friend of Tabashnick. Posing for his photograph on the rear of an automobile in 1947, he is located outside the Riverside Gardens at the corner of Auburn and Leverett Streets. (Courtesy of the West End Historical Association.)

Burrill Hill Tower, Lynn. Woods, Lynn, Mass.

Steel Tower on Burrill Hill was built in 1895 to aid in fire detection, but it incidentally provided spectacular views of the surrounding towns. The highest point in Lynn at 275 feet above sea level, Burrill Hill was briefly known during the 19th century by the fanciful name of Mount Nebo. Its original name was later returned.

Norwood's first ambulance appears in this early 1900s view, with its owner John Gillooly at the wheel. Founder of Gillooly's Funeral Home, he lived and practiced undertaking at 126 Walpole Street. This photograph was taken in front of George Metcalf's house next door. Norwood's 1911 Directory advertised Gillooly's "coaches, ambulances, hearses, and automobiles to let, office 605 Washington Street."

# Two
# TO SERVE AND PROTECT

Members of the Hyde Park police force pose on the steps of the Hyde Park Library in 1910. From left to right are: (in front) Captain Robert Grant and Lieutenant Edward Welch; (first row) Alexander Herring, Frank Whitticker, Edward Sheppard, W. Runnels, George Tucker, and O. McMahon; (back row) William Downey, Andrew Cullen, Eldridge Dyer, Thomas Meighan, and Rodger Flaherty.

This view of the Chestnut Hill Avenue Fire Station shows firefighters and horse-drawn apparatus in 1902. The building was destroyed by fire in the late 1930s. In the early 1940s, its shell was incorporated into the Brighton Municipal Building, which was later converted into the Veronica Smith Senior Center.

Members of the Cambridge Police Department of 1915 pose on the steps of police headquarters in Central Square. From three constables in 1845, the Cambridge Police Department has grown into a professional department serving a major city.

Throughout the late 19th and early 20th centuries, Lynn struggled with the familiar problem of overcrowded schools. The construction of Lynn Classical in 1911, "a beautiful and commodious building . . . one of the best high school plants in the state," solved the problem for many years, at least at the high school level.

By 1931 the Nahant Police Department had grown from a force of one in 1878 to nine. George Burnett (left), John D. O'Connor (center), and Chief Larkin pose at the police station on Nahant Road with the new 1936 ambulance. (Courtesy Paul Wilson.)

The area across from Copp's Hill became a tangled wreck of wood-framed sheds and buildings, iron fences, and debris that was swept toward the edge of the Charles River by the force of the cascading molasses. (Courtesy of *The Boston Globe*.)

Chief of Police William Fred Wiggin was promoted to chief from patrolman in 1896 and served as chief from 1896 to 1899, when he was transferred to the night force.

Here, Peabody Police
Riot Squad, including
Police Chief Joseph
Donlon, practice their
riot control techniques.

A police chief and his driver stop in front of Police Station No. 1 in their Buick police car
about 1905. To the left of the policeman standing against the car is the entrance to the
Central Fire Station. Notice the hand-operated bell mounted to the hood of the police
car—a swift pull to the rope sounded their approach! (Courtesy of the West End Historical
Association.)

The members of the Boston Police Department assigned to Police Station No. 3 pose for a group portrait about 1895 in front of police headquarters. (Courtesy of the West End Historical Association.)

Cedar Grove Cemetery was laid out by Luther Briggs Jr. in the 1860s as an arboretum cemetery. On the banks of the Neponset River, Cedar Grove was originally known as "Gin Plain," as junipers in the area produced berries that could be used in the distillation of gin. The fountain, stately trees, and well-kept grounds still offer a place for nature walks.

A group of nurses and training nurses poses for a formal portrait at the turn of the century. White caps denoted registered nurses, while black-banded caps denoted student nurses. (Courtesy of the Massachusetts General Hospital.)

The Village Congregational Church was at the corner of River and Old Morton Streets, just a couple of blocks west of Washington Street. This simple church was later enlarged, but after World War II it disbanded and joined the Milton Congregational Church.

Firemen ascend ladders mounted against houses on Monument Avenue between Main and Warren Streets. The steep rise of Monument Avenue, with the sleek shaft of the Bunker Hill Monument crowning the top of Breed's Hill, can be seen in the background. (Courtesy of Bill Nolan.)

Members of the Hyde Park Fire Department pose in 1905 outside the Central Fire Station. From left to right are: (front row) John McDougald, Chief John Wetherbee, and Frank Kunkel; (back row) Edward Bullard, William McDougald, Michael Foley, Dennis Mahoney, and Frank Mercer.

Hyde Park firemen pose with their Amoskeag fire engine in Grew's Woods in 1890. On the left one of the firemen holds a silver trumpet, used not just as a ceremonial badge of office but also for shouting orders during a fire.

The Mineral Spring Hotel, built in 1810 in Glenmere, was purchased by Richard S. Fay and remodeled into one of the city's most elegant homes. Mr. Fay indulged his passions for gardening, ornamental trees, and sheep farming on his 500-acre estate. The home is seen in its declining years after the death of his widow, Madame Fay. It was torn down in 1916.

This is a group photograph of uniformed members of Steamer 2, Peabody. An interesting part of the uniform is the white leather belt emblazoned with the city's name.

Hunneman & Company produced the first American suction engine in 1833 on Hunneman Street in Roxbury. William C. Hunneman had built a tub in 1822, known as "The Phillips," which was used to fight fires with water that filled from fire buckets, but the later Hunneman steamers proved to be not only more efficient but an advanced form of firefighting. (Courtesy of the West Roxbury Historical Society.)

One of Roxbury's greatest sons was James Michael Curley (1874–1958), shown here with Thomas Norton Hart (right), a former mayor of Boston. Photographed at Boston City Hall in 1923, Curley would be elected mayor of Boston four times. The son of immigrants from Ireland, Curley would later serve in Congress and as governor of Massachusetts.

Members of the Roxbury City Guard pose in the Public Garden on September 13, 1870, in front of Thomas Ball's equestrian statue of George Washington. The townhouses in the background were built on Beacon Street, the former Mill Dam, and those on the left were built on Arlington Street after 1859, when the infilling of the Back Bay was commenced. (Courtesy of The Boston Athenaeum.)

Sailors parade past the State House on Flag Day, June 15, 1913. (Photograph by Leslie Jones, courtesy BPL.)

The Charlestown City Guard, Company D, 4th Regiment, Light Infantry succeeded the Company B, Charlestown Light Infantry, in 1846. Captain Francis Meredith Jr. is seated in the center of the first row with First Lieutenant Fred McDonald and Second Lieutenant Henry Y. Gilson on either side.

These young schoolgirls were enrolled in "domestic science," a course offered in the Boston Public School that stressed sewing, cooking, and associated "sciences." Posing in the kitchen of the Harvard School, they wore mop caps and aprons while learning of the art of making breads and cakes.

Gilda Pisapia and Joseph Sammarco were married on April 18, 1948, at the Our Lady of Mount Carmel Church on Gove Street. They leave the church followed by Mary Malio, her maid of honor, and Anthony Sammarco, his best man, as family and friends shower the newlyweds with confetti. (Courtesy of the Sammarco Family.)

Three residents of Hyde Park pose in their uniforms in 1904 during the National Encampment of the Grand Army of the Republic in Boston. From left to right are: Frank E. Conley (a veteran of the Spanish American War), Robert McKeown (a veteran of the Civil War), and Albert C. Clapp (a veteran of the Mexican War).

Officers of the Heavy Artillery, Company C, pose around one of the cannons of Fort Warren on George's Island. The huge cannon balls stacked on either side would surely wreak havoc when fired upon enemy ships. Notice the woman, probably an officer's wife, on the upper right. (Courtesy of the Boston Athenaeum.)

The Fife and Drum Corps of Camp #146, Sons of Veterans, pose on the steps of the Hyde Park Library on Memorial Day 1905. In their dapper uniforms, they were a popular group a century ago.

Lynn's first Catholic residents, present at least as early as the 1790s, had to attend services either in the Salem church or in private homes until St. Mary's parish was founded in 1862.

Posing for a group portrait in Burke's Funeral Home on Chambers Street in 1946 are, from left to right, as follows: (front row) John Sullivan, Edward Fitzgerald, William Hunter, Charles Chivakos, Robert Downes, Joseph Kenny, and Warren Lufkin; (back row) John Bartholomew, John Beaujang, Robert Corrano, Daniel Leary, Robert Burke, Charles Emmons, and Frank McCoy. (Courtesy of the West End Historical Association.)

# *Three*
# ETHNIC BOSTON

North Street in Boston's North End was decorated for All Saint's Day, June 23, 1929. Parades, pageants, and Saints Day observations have long played an important part in the social and religious life of Boston's Italian community. (Courtesy of the Boston Public Library.)

This 1914 photograph was taken in front of the studio of photographer Pietro Tisei in North Square (center left), at the heart of the downtown Italian enclave. Tisei immigrated to Boston from Tivoli, near Rome, before 1900 and settled in Somerville. To the left of the Tisei studio stood a telegraphic office and, to the right, an Italian pastry shop. In the open car in the foreground sit Mr. Buoncuore, Pietro's wife, Maria, and their children, Caroline, Francis, and Ralph. (Courtesy of Marie Tisei.)

By 1930, more than half of the barbers listed in the Boston City Directory were Italians. Italian barbers were also numerous in the suburbs. This 1937 photograph is of Swampscott's Rosa Brothers and Joe Reed Barber Shop, an inter-ethnic partnership. (Courtesy of Sylvia Curato.)

Gaetano Panarello is dressed in as a Native American holding an American flag in this 1917 photograph, taken the year that the United States entered WWI. Italian Americans were eager to demonstrate their commitment to the cause. Gaetano was the son of Santi Panarello, who owned a large barbershop on Court Street in the downtown. The Panarellos were residents of suburban Jamaica Plain in 1917. (Courtesy of Marge [Panarello] DiSciullo.)

John Tocci, a successful Newton contractor, who immigrated to Boston from San Donato val di Comino around 1910, is shown here in 1927 with his pregnant wife Virginia (Di Gregorio) Tocci, and their ten children, arranged by age. The children, from left to right, are as follows: Geraldine, Francis, Germania, Antoinette, Angelo, Laura, Anna and Lucy (twins), Valentino (in a sailor's suit), Concetta, and Jean (the baby on the floor). The last of their eleven children, Esther, was born a few months later. (Courtesy of James Cummings.)

In a photograph labeled, "A portion of the July Quota," we see immigrants from the Adriatic (probably from the port of Trieste) landing at the East Boston Immigration Station on July 23, 1923. This was just before the rigid new immigration laws went into effect that cut Italian immigration by more than 95 percent and put an end to the Great Migration. (Courtesy of the Boston Public Library.)

Four of the five Marchi brothers appear in this 1915 photograph, taken at Ten Hills in East Somerville. Caesar is the third from the left seated, with his hat on his knee, Battista is seated to the right of Caesar, Eugenio is seated at the extreme right, and Gianneto is the one standing farthest to the right. Battista, the eldest, owned and operated the Florence Restaurant in Downtown Boston. Cesare was later killed in WWI, and Somerville's Marchi Park was named in his honor. A fifth brother, Peter Marchi, does not appear in this photo. (Courtesy of Marie [Marchi] Bonello.)

Chef Edward Bonello (extreme right) is seen here in the kitchen of Boston's Parker House Restaurant. (Courtesy of Marie [Marchi] Bonello.)

Religious processions were held wherever Italians settled in significant numbers. This 1955 view is of the St. Alfio Procession on Common Street in Lawrence. (Courtesy of Jimmy [Bono] Geany.)

In a climate of severely limited opportunities, many Italian Americans sought advancement through competitive sports. Here we see Rocky Marciano (born Rocco Marchegiano) of Brockton, who in 1952 won the world heavyweight boxing championship, retiring undefeated in 1956. Rocky's father, Perrino Marchegiano, had emigrated from Chieti, a fishing village in the Abruzzi, before WWI. He settled in Brockton and worked in the shoe industry. The fighter's mother, Pasquelina Picchiutto, came to America from San Bartolomeo, near Naples, in 1918.

William Cardinal O'Connell arranged for Sister Mary Valentina, a teacher at St. Anthony's School in the North End and a member of the Order of Missionary Franciscan Sisters of the Immaculate Conception, to serve as Superior of the Home for Italian Children. Members of that order also staffed the facility. This early 1920s view shows the children enjoying the plants and flowers on the grounds of the Jamaica Plain property. (Courtesy of the Italian Home for Children.)

Large-scale emigration from Italy resumed after WWI and peaked in 1920, the last year of open immigration. This photograph is of Vincenzo Bonsignore in the uniform of a WWI Italian soldier, with his brother, before his emigration from Enna, Sicily. Vincenzo settled in East Cambridge in the early 1920s and opened a shoe repair shop on Cambridge Street. (Courtesy of Anthony Ricciardi.)

# B O S T O N

John Fitzgerald, a former mayor of Boston known as "Honey Fitz," and his friend Sir Thomas Lipton pose in front of the entrance to the Copley Plaza Hotel in 1923.

Newly arrived immigrants to Boston, *c.* 1900, were photographed on the Steerage deck of a ship. Notice the dichotomy between the women—those on the left wear fashionable hats and dark day dresses, while those on the right wear traditional head scarves and costumes. The steerage class for these ships was literally a "Tower of Babel" with the number of languages spoken.

These two Italian children sit on a suitcase that is propped up on a large trunk. The girl wears a cap with a ribbon of the ship, *Milano*, while the boy's cap is of the ship *Andrea Doria*.

A group of friends are playing bocci at the North End Park in the 1940s. Bocci, a game of bowls, has been played by Italians for centuries. (Courtesy of the Pizzeria Regina North End.)

Morris Rosen appearing in *Bar Kochba*. In 1918, when this portrait was taken, the Hebrew school was just six years old. The school was under the sponsorship of the Congregation Sons of Israel. (Photograph courtesy North Shore Jewish Historical Society.)

The First Congregational Church at South Common and Vine Streets was built in 1877 after its former edifice burned on Christmas Day in 1870. It served until 1944, when the parish merged with the North Congregational Church. It is headquartered on Lynnfield Street today.

Standing outside Fox's Pharmacy at the corner of Grove and Phillips Streets in the early 1940s are, from the left, "Bunny" Leonard, Dick Oliver, Bert Perkins, and Fred "Tut" Johnson. (Courtesy of the West End Historical Association.)

Smiling for the camera are, from left to right, Linda, Joyce, and Bill Crooks Jr. (Courtesy of the West End Historical Association.)

Richard Cardinal Cushing, gazing towards the open sea, stands erect with his miter and staff of office. A graduate in 1921 of Saint John's Seminary, he was elevated to the title of cardinal in 1958 by Pope John XXIII, and is shown here resplendent in vestments of silk and fine lace. Those who came to hear him also arrived by yacht and, in the foreground, by rowboat. (Courtesy SBHS.)

Iroquois Indians pose in full regalia on the stops of the Craigie-Longfellow House in 1910. Their visit to the former home of the great writer Henry Wadsworth Longfellow proved to be both an interesting and a uniquely colorful one.

John F. Kennedy is in his Halloween costume, about age nine, in the rear of his Abbottsford Road home. The Kennedy family lived here from 1921 to 1927. Robert F. Kennedy was born here, as were Eunice and Patricia. (Courtesy of John F. Kennedy Library.)

# Four
# BOSTON IN MOTION

Saint James Street was a busy thoroughfare in 1913, with streetcars passing every few minutes destined for all parts of the city. On the left is the corner of Trinity Church, with the Hotel Westminster next to the Copley Plaza. The Hotel Westminster was demolished when the John Hancock Tower was built.

A horse-drawn sleigh passes the Commonwealth Avenue Mall at Berkeley Street about 1885. In the distance can be seen the spire of the Brattle Square Church, now the First Baptist Church in Boston.

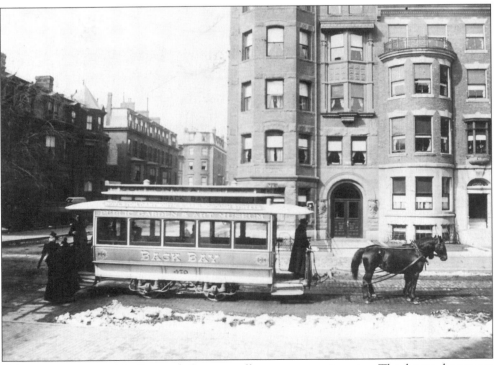

A horse car stops on Marlborough Street to allow passengers to enter. This horse-drawn car was to serve the Back Bay until December 24, 1899, when the line was retired from service. (Courtesy of David Rooney.)

Fred M. Chase was intrepid, to say the least. The first automobile owner in town also became the first local to purchase an airplane in 1919. As the photographer of the 1897 pictures taken from the Unitarian church steeple, his thirst for aerial views was an established fact in town.

Fred M. Chase is pictured here in the town's first automobile, a one-cylinder "Locomobile".

In the early years of this century, the Commonwealth Avenue streetcar line ran all the way to Newton's Norumbega Park, an amusement park that the street railway company established to attract riders. This 1910 view shows a streetcar taking on passengers at Commonwealth and Lake Streets (now the end of the line). (Collection of Kevin T. Farrell.)

Women sailors salute from the swan boats in May 1937. (Photograph by Leslie Jones, courtesy BPL.)

This *c*. 1860 albumen print of Otis's third house shows a horse-drawn sled waiting in front. In 1828, the mansion was the scene of the owner's inauguration as mayor of Boston. Today the mansion houses the American Meteorological Society. (Photograph by Thomas Marr, courtesy SPNEA.)

Grove Hall, the junction of Blue Hill Avenue and Warren and Washington Streets, was not always the busy square it became in later years. In this 1893 view, we are looking down Blue Hill Avenue as a trolley arrives from Sullivan Square in Charlestown. There is no explanation for the horse-drawn rig standing on the car tracks.

During the winter months when snow covered many streets for weeks at a time, sled runners replaced the wheels on many omnibuses, such as this one at Boylston Street in 1899, in front of the Boston Public Library. This coach was in use on the Marlborough Street Horse Car Line, which often went unplowed after winter storms. On the right is the new Old South Church, designed by Cummings and Sears and built in 1874.

Many of Boston's omnibuses, rendered obsolete by the advent of the electric trolleys, found second careers serving passengers in suburban areas such as this coach sold to an operator in Swampscott, viewed on May 22, 1901.

The Boston Elevated equipped several of its surface cars, including one "Type Four" car, as traveling classrooms providing refresher courses to employees on the electrical and braking equipment on the cars they operated. Here is one group of eager students aboard the trainer "Type Four" car, which was equipped with a movie projector and electrical equipment.

Beginning in 1986, Boston's MBTA began taking delivery of the new "Type 7" articulated cars, which replaced the last of the 42-year-old PCC cars. The "Type 7," built by Kinski-Sharyo of Japan, have proven to be high quality, rugged, and comfortable cars. This scene is at Waban Station on the Highland Branch.

From 1895 through 1915, the U.S. Mail was carried on special cars between the main post office and branch postal stations. The cars were painted white with red and gilt lettering and had the right-of-way over all other street traffic along with police and fire vehicles. This view was taken in Post Office Square, Boston, in May of 1907.

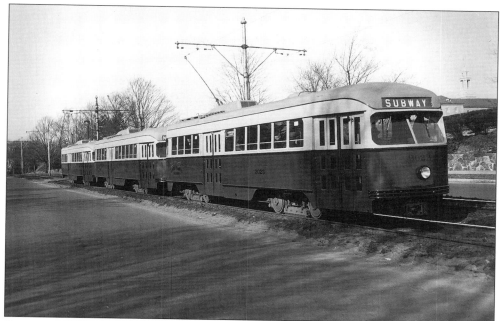

Between 1940 and 1951, the Boston system purchased over 300 "PCC Type" cars, most of which were used to replace the center door trolleys on the Green Line routes. Although fast and comfortable, the "PCC" cars, seen here on Commonwealth Avenue, could not handle heavy crowds as well as the center door cars they replaced.

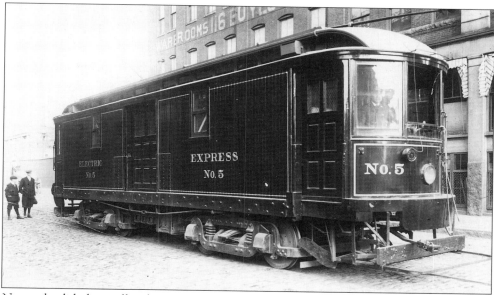

Not only did the trolley lines provide passenger and mail service but also freight and package express service between Boston, Worcester, Springfield, Brockton, and Fall River, MA, and Newport and Providence, RI, as well as other points. Here is an electric freight car of the Bay State Street Railway on Harrison Avenue in Boston in November 1922.

Let's strike up the band, the Al Moore Band that is, for the 1921 Public Safety Awareness Campaign. The practice of using an open streetcar festooned with advertising messages and carrying a brass band was a longtime Boston custom, dating from the horse car days. Al Moore is the gentleman in the suit in the center.

From 1927 until 1930, Boston Elevated operated an extra fare (25¢) deluxe bus line from Beacon Street in Brookline to Scollay Square in Boston. The regular bus fare was 10¢. Just look at all those fashionable fur coats!

The Dudley Street Station was photographed on September 17, 1901, with trolley cars and an elevated train entering the station, which within a decade would become one of the busiest terminals in the United States.

This view of the elevated train passenger platform at the Dudley Street Station shows the amount of effort expended to provide an attractive as well as efficient station. Note the thoughtful use of mahogany, leaded glass, and brass trim in the station.

In April 1938, the Boston Elevated Company introduced speedy, quiet electric trolleybuses on the route from Harvard Square to Huron and Aberdeen Avenues. This photograph shows a Huron Avenue trolleybus in the Harvard Square Tunnel Station. Cambridge is still served by these smooth, quiet, fume-free vehicles. (Courtesy of Frank Cheney.)

Col. Thomas Wentworth Higginson (1823–1911) and his daughter Margaret (Mrs. James Dellinger Barney) pose for their photograph astride a three-wheeled bicycle. Higginson was the first colonel of a black regiment in the Civil War and was the author of *Army Life in a Black Regiment, Atlantic Essays, Common Sense About Women, The Afternoon Landscape*, and numerous other books. His essay in the *Atlantic Monthly* entitled "Ought Women to Learn the Alphabet?" was so thought provoking that it is credited as the seed from which Smith College grew.

In the summer of 1892, crew members of this trolley on the long Bowdoin Square-Harvard Square-Arlington Heights line stopped long enough to have their picture taken on North Avenue. In 1901, a state law mandated closed ends for trolley cars, thereby providing protection from the cold weather for motormen, as car operators were called. (Courtesy of Frank Cheney.)

This view of the Harvard Bridge looks south toward Boston's Back Bay. Notice the streetcar crossing the bridge at the lower left.

The Christopher Gibson School was built on School Street and named for an early settler of Dorchester who had left a bequest to the town to benefit the schools. Designed by Boston architect Gridley J. Fox Bryant, this Italianate school stood in marked contrast to the one-room schoolhouse of a generation earlier.

The plush interior of Car 101 was a sea of green velvet, silk, and brass trimmings. General Bancroft traveled as far afield as Beverly Cove, Springfield, and Newport, RI, in this luxurious parlor car, which ended up as a roadside restaurant in Attleboro, MA.

Here is the interior of the same mail car showing the sorting tables, bins, canceling machines, and mail sacks. The mail was sorted and canceled as the cars traveled between the post offices, saving a great amount of time.

The ship *Panay* was built in 1877 by J. Taylor of East Boston. (Courtesy of the BPL.)

A group of "First Cabin" passengers sailing for Liverpool, England, pose on the deck of the ship *Pavonia*. Well and warmly dressed, the passengers seem prepared for the ocean winds, a rolling ship, and hopefully an enjoyable passage. (Courtesy of the BPL.)

From its inception the Harvard Bridge was a heavily traveled artery, as evidenced in this c. 1925 photograph. In this photograph, we see the Cambridge shore in the background, with the Riverbank Court apartments to the left and the main buildings of the Massachusetts Institute of Technology to the right.

Officers of the ship *Pavonia* were photographed on board in 1892. From left to right are as follows: (seated) First Officer Cresser, Chief Officer Inman, Chief Engineer Foulds, and Second Engineer Coutts; (standing) Fourth Officer Highes, Engineer Allsop, Engineer Grindley, Third Engineer Campbell, Engineer Paynton, and Third Officer Kidley. (Courtesy of the BPL.)

Workmen take a break on Lewis Street in the summer of 1900 as they dig the underwater tunnel that would connect East Boston to downtown Boston. (Courtesy of SPNEA.)

With picks and shovels these workmen prepare the tunnel in Maverick Square in the summer of 1900. A team of horses dredge the rough base surface as the wood-framed supports are erected for the roof of the tunnel. (Courtesy of SPNEA.)

Two boys stand on the arch of the East Boston tunnel as a streetcar emerges at Maverick Square.

A train passes through the tunnel built under Jeffries Point by the Boston, Revere Beach and Lynn Railroad. The mansard-roofed house above the tunnel is on Sumner Street in East Boston. (Courtesy of the Lynn Historical Society.)

A crowded ferry approaches the East Boston waterfront in the 1920s. The North Ferry left from Battery Wharf on Commercial Street in Boston and docked at Border Street; the South Ferry left from State Street and docked at Lewis Street. Many of the passengers would continue on by train to Revere Beach via the Boston, Revere Beach and Lynn Railroad for an afternoon of amusements and swimming. (Courtesy of the BPL.)

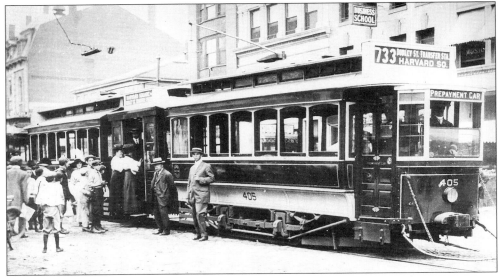

Service on today's Green Line in Boston is supplied by modern articulated cars, as it is on many light-rail systems worldwide. The articulated design enables cars to bend in the middle as they go around corners. The now popular design was developed in May 1912 by John Lindall, chief equipment engineer of the Boston Elevated Company, one of whose early articulated cars is seen here on Massachusetts Avenue at Central Square, en route to Dudley Street in Roxbury. (Courtesy of Frank Cheney.)

In 1924, eager passengers board a Massachusetts Avenue Fageol Safety Coach, used on the route from Central Square in Cambridge to the Cottage Farm Bridge. Frank Fageol was one of the pioneer bus manufacturers in the United States, and his company remained in business until *c.* 1960. (Courtesy of Frank Cheney.)

A streetcar bound for Chelsea emerges from the tunnel at Maverick Square about 1908. Streetcars could travel from East Boston to downtown Boston in seven minutes via the first underwater tunnel in the country. On the right can be seen a corner of the Maverick House. (Courtesy of SPNEA.)

The Congress Street Bridge was built in 1899 to replace a wooden bridge, and it still serves as a major route from South Boston into Boston. Note the reversed date in the bridge overhead.

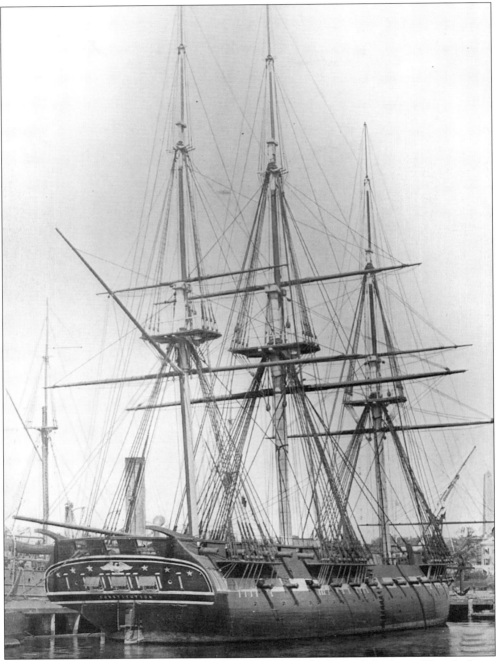

The *USS Constitution* was designed by Joshua Humphreys and built in Hartt's (now Constitution) Wharf in Boston's North End. Launched in 1797, the *Constitution* was to serve the country well—especially in battle with the British ship *Guerriere*. Here she lies at berth in the former Boston Navy Yard in Charlestown, in the shadow of the Bunker Hill Monument, visible on the right.

Streetcars are pulled up on East First Street near City Point in the 1940s. In the distance is the present-day entrance to the Conley Marine Terminal. (Courtesy SBHS.)

The Commonwealth Dock Head House was built in 1912 under the direction of the Port of Boston. An impressive dock, whose slogan was "Sail From Boston," it was 1,200 feet long, and was built to "accommodate at one time any two of the largest ocean steamships afloat and also two or three smaller vessels." Today, it is the World Trade Center.

The car barns and storage facilities of the Massachusetts Bay Transit Authority were located on East First Street. The streetcar shown here is turning in the yard and will exit the gates onto East First Street. On either side of the entrance are piers surmounted by unusually attractive art deco lights. (Courtesy SBHS.)

This 1891 view of Tremont Street, looking south with the Park Street Church on the right and the old Horticultural Hall on the left, was taken from the Tremont House. Most of the streetcars in this photograph are horse-drawn ones, with only a few electric cars in sight. This section of Tremont Street had three tracks to handle the heavy streetcar traffic.

A feature of the trolley subway was the Information Booth, the only one on the entire system, which was located at the Park Street Station on the southbound platform. (Courtesy of David Rooney.)

The 80-foot, 90-ton dragger *Valiant* was built by Raymond Palombo and Frank McClain Jr. in the yard between their homes on Forty Steps Lane over a six-year period. The move toward Tudor Wharf in October 1963 provided excitement for the whole town, culminating in the ship's christening by ten-year-old Alma Palombo. In the foreground are Alfred Arzillo (left) and Robert Enzenger. Officer Joseph Flynn, Louis Le Tourneau (in the knit cap), and an unidentified neighbor discuss the event. The *Valiant* later sank 70 miles east of Nantucket with no loss of life.

# *Five*
# GREATER BOSTON

The charity bazaar at Holm Lea included food and clothing booths, games, and sideshows like Punch and Judy. The swan boats from the Boston Public Garden were also imported to Sargent's Pond for the day. (Courtesy of BPL.)

# BOSTON

This photograph was taken in the main reading room of the Holton Library in 1968.

A gallery of the Museum of Fine Arts had many of the paintings that still grace the galleries of the present museum. Art students pose on the right, resting from their labors of copying the original paintings.

Taking part in a parade of Boston suffragettes in 1914 were, from the left, Helen Keller, her secretary Pauline Thompson, and her teacher, Mrs. J.A. Macy. In the background is the facade of Trinity Church in Copley Square.

The lagoon had been planted with weeping willows that gracefully arched over the edge of the pond. During the winter, the pond was flooded and allowed to freeze and was swiftly "covered by a gay throng of happy youth, whose skates glisten in the sun and whose merry voices ring out joyously on the air." This photograph looks from the area near the corner of Boylston and Arlington Streets.

By the late 1940s, Kenmore Square was a busy intersection with buses travelling along Beacon Street and Brookline Avenue and the subway running under Commonwealth Avenue. The large apartment building at the center was designed by E.B. Stratton and built in 1923. The Kenmore Square Garage on the far left and the double-parked cars along Commonwealth Avenue on the right foreshadow today's dependency on the automobile. (Courtesy of David Rooney.)

Henry James, well-known writer of the late nineteenth century, once declared that Mount Vernon was "the only respectable street in America." (Photograph by Leslie Jones, courtesy BPL.)

Four young ladies ice skate on the Public Garden's frozen lagoon. (Photograph by Leslie Jones, courtesy BPL.)

Six ladies enjoy lunching on the Common, *c.* 1908. (Courtesy *Boston Herald.*)

Young children pose on a captured German gun on the Common. (Photograph by Leslie Jones, courtesy BPL.)

The one-time "Old Boston Days on Beacon Hill" celebration on June 16, 1924, was a historical fete that set the clock back one hundred years and benefited the Women's Municipal League. The day was dedicated to old-time pageantry, costumes, and music. Masses of people lined up to enjoy the parade at Louisburg Square. (Photograph by Leslie Jones, courtesy BPL.)

The Great Blizzard of 1888 blanketed the city with a deep pile of snow. Through the snow-laden and ice-adorned trees of the Boston Common, we can just make out the State House. The storm was so severe and the snowfall so heavy that the trees look as if they are bowing to the capitol!

On Class Day, June 16, 1914, members of the Harvard Class of 1864 marched to Harvard Stadium past the Weld Boathouse, which had been designed by Peabody and Stearns and built in 1907 through the generosity of George Walker Weld. Class members are, from left to right, James T. Bixby, Henry A. Parker, Edward Russell Cogswell, Woodward Emery, and Edward Blake Robins, holding the class flag.

Central Square was literally the center of East Boston when it was laid out by the East Boston Company. The junction of Meridien, Porter, Bennington, Saratoga, Border, and Liverpool Streets, it has a circular tree-shaded park on the left. Streetcars approached Central Square on Meridien Street. The stores on the right included Walcott & Company, the Central Hat Company, and the Morrison Grocery Company. (Courtesy of SPNEA.)

Lexington Street connects Meridien and East Eagle Streets on Eagle Hill. Note the streetcar tracks laid down the center of the street in this turn-of-the-century photograph. (Courtesy of SPNEA.)

John Fitzgerald Kennedy campaigned in the North End in the late 1940s for a seat in Congress. Standing beneath the equestrian statue of Paul Revere, an attentive crowd surrounds the future senator and president. (Courtesy of the BPL.)

Looking north from the Copp's Hill Burying Ground, the Bunker Hill Monument rises above houses closely built along the Hull Street side of the cemetery. On this ground the British batteries were erected that destroyed Charlestown on June 17, 1775.

Parishioners speak with a priest on the steps of Saint Stephen's Church. These stairs were removed during the restoration of the church, which was undertaken by Richard Cardinal Cushing in 1964–65. (Courtesy of the BPL.)

In the 1930s, children and adults cool off during a hot summer day at the North End Park. (Courtesy of the BPL.)

On June 1, 1967, Senator Edward M. Kennedy visited the North End Branch of the Boston Public Library to view an exhibit on the history of the North End. "Honey Fitz" (his maternal grandfather), Mayor John F. Fitzgerald, and Rose Fitzgerald Kennedy (his mother) were born in the North End and were once parishioners of Saint Stephen's Church on Hanover Street. Greeting Senator Kennedy are Reverend Sullivan of Saint Stephen's Church and Librarian Mrs. Geraldine Herrick. (Courtesy of the BPL.)

Clark's Pharmacy was located at 500 Washington Street on the north end of the Conger Block. Established c. 1900, this beautiful ornamental soda fountain was the last of its kind in Norwood. Shown here are Madge Clark and her mother.

A domestic arts teacher stands before her students, who are preparing food over burners in the Charlestown High School. With long aprons covering their dresses and caps over their hair, these girls learned various recipes that could be tried out at home.

A "tramp resting under tree" was photographed at the turn of the century outside the Kettell House at Adams and Chestnut Streets. With a shady tree, and an obviously sun-dappled afternoon, who could resist such a temptation? (Courtesy of the BPL.)

This c. 1900 view of children swimming on the shore of the polluted Charles River in Brighton, opposite the Perkins Institute for the Blind, underscores the desperate need for recreational facilities for working-class families that then existed in the basin area.

This panoramic view of the Harvard University buildings on the Cambridge side of the Charles shows Winthrop House (left), the first Harvard building to open to the river, designed by Shepley, Rutan, & Coolidge and dating from 1913. Winthrop House's courtyard was inspired by England's Hampton Court Palace. To the right lies Dunster House. At the extreme left we see a portion of the Weeks Bridge, linking the Cambridge campus to the business school complex in Allston.

Looking south from Central Square, Meridien Street leads to Maverick Square. A horse drinks from the horse trough on the left and the spire of the Maverick Congregational Church can be seen rising above the trees in the park. (Courtesy of SPNEA.)

Meridien Street, seen here looking north from the corner of Havre Street, had numerous stores of every description on both sides of the street. (Courtesy of SPNEA.)

Two boys doff their jackets as they walk down the main walk, east at Wood Island Park. The harbor can be seen through the trees in the distance. (Courtesy of SPNEA.)

Miss Ray's room at the Princeton Grammar School posed for their class picture in 1896.
(Courtesy of the BPL.)

On the "tenth and a half birthday of Mary Poppins" (May 1946), children acted out the
play and pose proudly in front of their audience. (Courtesy of the BPL.)

A Boston Red Sox baseball team tribute was held in Peabody in 1967. Seated in the back seat of the Ford convertible are Dick and Norma Williams and Mayor Edward Meaney. The United States Marine Corps certainly had the crowd under control.

These friends bicycled to Grew's Woods at the turn of the century. While their companions lounge on the ground, the ladies pose with a Columbia bicycle.

Members of the basketball team of Hyde Park High School pose in 1909 with their coach, who is on the far right in the back row.

Water Street was photographed in the winter of 1895 from Fairmount Avenue looking toward Dana Avenue. The street would not be plowed but "rolled": a heavy roller was pulled by horses to pack the snow for sleighs.

The office of Master Edward W. Schuerch of the Bowditch School had a roll-top oak desk and an entire wall lined with overflowing bookcases.

Grace Hiler was a member of the Jamaica Plain Tuesday Club. She was photographed in London as a bridesmaid for a wedding. A faithful and active member of the club, she bequeathed a large sum of money to further its goals. (Courtesy of the BPL.)

Described at the time of its construction in 1912 as "a thoroughly modern school building of the best type," the Brickett School is still in use.

The 250th Anniversary Committee of Milton met in October 1912 outside the town hall for this photograph. From the left to right are: John Alden Lee, Dr. Freeland D. Lillie, Nathaniel T. Kidder, Arthur H. Tucker, and Andrew H. Ward.

Edward Everett Hale (1822–1909) addressed members of the First Parish Church after services on July 12, 1908. Hale, a nephew of Governor Edward Everett, served as chaplain of the United States Senate and was the retired minister of the South Congregational Church in Boston. (Courtesy of the BPL.)

Henry Colby Wilson was a long-term town selectman. He is seen here in Dorothy's Cove, headed toward Tudor Beach in his well-beloved *Widgeon*. Tudor Wharf is out of view to the right in this 1890s panorama of the waterfront at Tudor Beach between Winter Street and Summer Street. The town clock in the steeple of the Village Church on Nahant Road was very important in town life and was specifically placed high so that it could be seen from a great distance both on land and from the sea.

The landing of the South Boston Yacht Club was a popular place to loll on a summer afternoon, or to take a small boat that would allow you to get to your yacht at anchor in the harbor. This bucolic turn-of-the-century scene shows how popular yachting had become in South Boston, but also how attractive the area of City Point was to residents and visitors alike. (Courtesy SBHS.)

These young women are members of the Athletic Association of the Roxbury Memorial High School for Girls in 1928. From left to right are as follows: (seated) Sylvia Minnucci, Esther Bassick, Marjorie Spinney, and Michelina Rizzo; (standing) Eunice Lahaise, Muriel Kodis, and Helen Jackson. (Courtesy of Mary A. Connell.)

A remarkably well-dressed student, complete with a straw bonnet, weeds a vegetable patch in the George Putnam Grammar School garden. These experimental gardens eventually led to the Victory Gardens that were cultivated during World War I and World War II.

The Weston School for Girls was a private academy for young ladies at 37–43 Saint James Street. A day and resident school, it fitted young ladies "for life as well as examinations."

Robert B. Williams (1829–1911) lived at 37 (now 67) Perrin Street and was a Boston merchant who dealt in tea. (Courtesy of the Williams Family.)

Some patients were thought so special that even television stars visited them while recuperating at the New England Baptist Hospital. Here, Rin Tin Tin sits on a sofa while visiting a young patient in 1956. (Courtesy of the New England Baptist Hospital.)

Children pose outside the entrance to the Aquarium in the 1940s. While it existed, school trips always included a visit to the Aquarium, where the excitement of seeing exotic and rare fish was almost as great as being out of school on a day trip!

At the turn of the century the L Street Bath House had bathing and swimming facilities, but after the new bath house was built, it had showers, saunas, and men and boys going au naturel on the beach.

The L Street Bath House was on Columbia Road, opposite L Street. A pedimented center pavilion of post and beam construction, it had flanking wings. This attractive bath house was later replaced by the brick and limestone bath house that is presently on the site.

South Boston, seen here from the floating Life Saving Station, created quite an impression at the turn of the century. (Courtesy SBHS.)

These young girls jump rope outside their homes in the West End in the 1950s. (Courtesy of the West End Historical Association.)

Father Powers participates in a May Procession on McLean Street in 1940. Father Powers was a popular priest at Saint Joseph's Church, and was well known throughout the West End by residents of all faiths. (Courtesy of the West End Historical Association.)

Scollay Square, named for 18th-century merchant John Scollay, was an active intersection at the turn of the century. The statue of Governor John Winthrop (1588–1649) on the right was sculpted by Horatio Greenough and was placed in the intersection, which was often referred to as Winthrop Square. The statue is today located in the Back Bay, in the garden of First and Second Church on Marlborough Street. (Courtesy of Frank Cheney.)

A group of boys stops for a quick game of "penny ante" in front of a small grocery store in the West End. (Courtesy of the West End Historical Association.)

Ensuring that the children in this May Procession march in formation and behave themselves is a nun in a traditional habit. (Courtesy of the West End Historical Association.)

Posing in front of Recko's Meat and Grocery Shop at the corner of Brighton and Chambers Streets in 1943 are, from left to right, Teddy Lupo, Walter Kozol, Bill Piniak, and Roland Phillips. (Courtesy of the West End Historical Association.)

The town landing in Milton as seen in 1897 from Godfrey's Wharf.

Photographed at the turn of the century, the Neponset River divided Dorchester (on the right) and Milton. The boathouse of John Collins and the former Preston Chocolate Mill can be seen on the right. In the distance, one can see the Hotel Milton, an inn located at the bridge crossing the Neponset River; it was here that the first local Catholic mass was said in 1840.

Looking east from Hutchinson Field on Adams Street to Milton Hill, the view toward the harbor is as panoramic and breathtaking today as it was a century ago. Blanketed with a fresh covering of snow, the hill rolls toward the marshes before reaching the harbor.

A group of East Milton women posed in 1864 for this photograph. From left to right are: Mrs. John Emerson, Miss Emma Emerson, Mrs. Hilary Bygrave, Miss Clara Babcock, Miss Susan Brokenshire, Mrs. Charles R. Young, Mrs. Albert A. Brackett, Miss M. Alice Babcock, and Mrs. Frederick M. Hamlin.

Work on a farm was hard and seemingly endless, but this worker manages to offer the camera an engaging smile.

Major General Grenville Dodge, Post 50, Grand Army of the Republic, proposed a memorial to the soldiers and sailors of the Civil War in 1879. The sum of $8,000 was procured by the town for its construction. The 50-foot high monument was constructed by the Hallowell Granite Company, and the dedication took place on November 10, 1881.

A 1954 photograph of downtown Peabody shows a thriving shopping district, bustling with activity. Note the many prominent stores, including W.T. Grant's, First National Stores, Raymond's Pharmacy, and A.H. Whidden & Sons.

Seated at a roadside stand at Five Corners, Lake, Pine, and Winona Streets, are the proprietors, Stuart and Clara A. Bell, c. 1927.

115

Pictured here are charming and lovely representatives of Holiday Bowling Lanes and North Shore Cinema, at Northshore Shopping Center. This publicity pose made it hard to resist patronization of these establishments.

On Sunday, May 16, 1954, heavy rains caused the bursting of a dam owned by Eastman Gelatine Corporation, flooding downtown Peabody. Foster Street, depicted here, was completely under water. Some areas were inundated by 6 feet of water.

Even the dog is interested in the photographer's subject, somewhere out in the hills of Arlington. This elaborate set up was necessary to obtain almost any kind of photograph in the days before higher-speed roll films.

Omar Whittemore and Jim Poland make an overnight camping excursion to Elizabeth Island in Spy Pond.

The Arlington Lawn Tennis Club was founded in 1883 when tennis was a comparatively new game in the United States. It was a rather genteel sport at first, adopted by the croquet-playing set from the neighboring estates on Pleasant Street.

Dorothy Homer (Chamberlain) serves up a ball on the courts of the Arlington Lawn Tennis Club.

# Six
# THE GREAT FIRE OF 1872

Shown here, "Boston In Flames" is a lithograph by Currier and Ives that depicts the city ablaze. The dome of the Massachusetts State House can be seen in the center with flames rising high into the evening sky. In the foreground are small boats, ferries, and excursion ships filled with spectators who watched as Boston was engulfed in flames.

Looking down Washington Street from Winter Street, firemen have cordoned off spectators as the fire ravages the buildings on the east side of Washington Street. In the center of the etching is the facade of Macullar, Williams and Parker Company, which surprisingly survived the fire. In the distance, at the corner of Milk Street, rises the spire of the Old South Meeting House.

The ruins of Shreve, Crump and Low on Summer Street near Washington Street were not the result of the fire but a gas explosion. On Sunday night, November 10, 1872, a second fire erupted as the underground gas pipes on Summer Street exploded, causing further destruction in the area now referred to as the "Burnt Out District." (Courtesy of David Rooney.)

The crenelated tower of Trinity Church rises from the rubble-strewn Summer Street on the morning after the fire was stopped. A group of men stand in front of what is now the corner of Summer and Washington Streets, and on the right are the ruins of the Mercantile Buildings at the corner of Summer and Hawley Streets. The studio of William Morris Hunt was also destroyed in the fire, along with his paintings and those of numerous European masters displayed in his studio. (Courtesy of David Rooney.)

The first buildings destroyed by the fire are visible in the center left on Kingston Street, looking from Summer Street.

A man walks past a building at the junction of High and Summer Streets that was one of the few to remain standing, though thoroughly gutted by the fire.

A group of merchants and their employees pose for their photograph among the ruins of their former places of business. The granite seemed to melt with the intensity of the heat, and the ruins on the right have a grotesque look to them.

The remaining portion of this granite facade looked like melted sugar candy after the effects of the fire. The intensity of the heat of the fire caused a large amount of the granite to literally melt, creating stark and grotesque shapes that projected from the ruins.

In this photograph, a man stands guard over a safe outside 25 Pearl Street. Many of the safes were recovered in the weeks following the fire, with some of the contents intact; however, for the most part safes fell through the floors to the cellars where they baked in the heat of the smoldering coals in furnace rooms.

125

From this angle looking north from Summer Street, one can see that the fire had levelled most of the downtown district. Columns have fallen on top of the granite and bricks that were once part of elegant commercial blocks. In the distance can be seen the tower of Trinity Church and the Park Street Church.

Summer Street was a desolate area that had little resemblance to its former appearance other than the cleared streets. Walls and chimneys rise from the ruins showing the extent of the destruction.

Standing on Milk Street, a group of men gaze at the ruins of the buildings in and around Liberty Square, near the Mason Building, where the fire was eventually stopped. (Courtesy of David Rooney.)

A panoramic view of the devastation wrought by the great fire, as seen from Purchase Street looking toward Summer and Washington Streets, was captured about a week after the fire was stopped. Woodsheds have been erected in the foreground, and most of the streets have been cleared of debris for ease of transportation. The dome of the Massachusetts State House can be seen on the right, flanked by the spires of the Park Street Church (on the left) and the Old South Meeting House.

127

After the fire, Summer Street was rebuilt with impressive buildings five and six stories in height. On the left is the former site of Church Green, the junction of Bedford and Summer Streets; the street on the right is Devonshire Street. In the distance is the spire of the Park Street Church. Horse-drawn delivery wagons line both sides of the thriving commercial district once known as the "Burnt District." (Courtesy of William Diwllon.)

In the years immediately after the fire, Summer Street became a major street, with offices and warehouses being built on the site of the mansions designed by Bulfinch. In the distance is the spire of the Park Street Church. (Courtesy of William Dillon.)